nickelodeon

ARE YOU SMARTER THAN A 5TH GRADER

HISTORY CLASS

A COMPANION QUIZ BOOK

TABLE OF CONTENTS

ARE YOU SMARTER THAN A 5TH GRADER

Welcome to *Are You Smarter Than a 5th Grader*! The show that gives grown-ups the chance to win $100,000 by testing their smarts and proving that they are smarter than a 5th grader.

To play, each contestant faces different subjects, starting with the 1st-Grade level and going all the way to the 5th-Grade level. Before each grade level begins, the contestant chooses one of their classmates to help.

The questions are taken straight from grade-school textbooks, randomly mixed among open-ended, multiple-choice, and true/false questions.

> 1st–2nd Grade: 1 question each
> 3rd–4th Grade: 2 questions each
>
> In 1st–4th Grade, the contestant receives 2 cheats: COPY and PEEK.

- If a contestant chooses to COPY, they use their classmate's answer, sight unseen.

- If a contestant chooses to PEEK, they are shown their classmate's answer and can choose to use that answer or not.

- If the contestant gets a question right, they earn the money at stake and move up the ladder. But if they get a question wrong, they stay at their current level, and continue on with their questions!

After all 1st- through 4th-Grade questions are asked, it's time for the 5th-Grade questions . . . and the chance to multiply the money a contestant has already won!

5th Grade: 5 questions to answer with 60 seconds on the clock. The right answers won't be revealed until all 5 answers are locked in!

- The money is multiplied 2×, 3×, 4×, 5×, 10× with each correct answer.

- If a contestant isn't confident with their answer, they have one cheat available to them. This is played just like a PEEK, where the contestant can go with their classmate's answer or choose one of their own, at which point we'll see if they are correct or not.

Now it's your turn to test your smarts! Turn the page and find out if you're smarter than a 5th grader!

$10,000

$5,000

$2,500

$1,000

$500

$250

MEET THE CLASSMATES

SAYA

FAVORITE SUBJECTS
- Vocabulary
- History

SKILLS / FACTS
- Contortionist
- Detailed character artist
- Speaks fluent Japanese

PATRICK

FAVORITE SUBJECTS
- Vocabulary
- Grammar

SKILLS / FACTS
- Fascinated by dinosaurs
- Plays the trumpet
- Kung Fu master

COLIN

FAVORITE SUBJECTS
- Social Studies
- Anatomy

SKILLS / FACTS
- Boxer
- Pinewood Derby car champ
- Champion swimmer

MIA

FAVORITE SUBJECTS
- Science
- English

SKILLS / FACTS
- Published poet
- Plays the harp
- Runs cross-country

TRISTAN

FAVORITE SUBJECTS
- History
- Math

SKILLS / FACTS
- Tae Kwon Do master
- Has pet bearded dragons
- Created a rap song about the show

COOPER

FAVORITE SUBJECTS
- Math
- Health

SKILLS / FACTS
- President of his class
- Juggler
- Push-up pro

AMIRA

FAVORITE SUBJECTS
- Reading
- Science

SKILLS / FACTS
- Wants to find life outside of Earth
- Wants to work for NASA
- Honor roll student

QUINNE

FAVORITE SUBJECTS
- Vocabulary
- Reading

SKILLS / FACTS
- Wants to be a roller coaster engineer
- Built a skate ramp in her yard
- Drummer in a band

JAMIR

FAVORITE SUBJECTS
- Grammar
- Science

SKILLS / FACTS
- Aspiring action star
- Has a funny nickname
- Bow tie fanatic

CHLOE

FAVORITE SUBJECTS
- Literature
- Math

SKILLS / FACTS
- Does stand-up comedy
- MMA champ
- Speaks Mandarin

NICK

FAVORITE SUBJECTS
- History
- Geography

SKILLS / FACTS
- Loves game shows
- Kayaker
- Hip-Hop dancer

ISABELLA

FAVORITE SUBJECTS
- Reading
- History

SKILLS / FACTS
- Salsa dancer
- Has won multiple pageants
- Loves sloths

FIRST GRADE

1 WHAT ARE THE LAST FIVE WORDS IN THE US PLEDGE OF ALLEGIANCE?

2 WHAT STATE WOULD YOU VISIT TO SEE ROCKY MOUNTAIN NATIONAL PARK?

3 WHAT IS THE ONLY OCEAN NAMED FOR A COUNTRY?

4 TRUE OR FALSE? NEW YORK CITY IS CLOSER TO THE PACIFIC OCEAN THAN THE ATLANTIC OCEAN.

5 THE ORIGINAL ENGLISH COLONISTS IN AMERICA SAILED ACROSS WHICH OCEAN TO REACH THEIR NEW HOMES?

6 WHAT IS THE ONLY US FEDERAL HOLIDAY THAT CANNOT FALL ON A MONDAY?

7 WHO WAS THE FIRST PERSON TO SIGN THE US DECLARATION OF INDEPENDENCE?

8 IF ISABELLA GOES SAILING ON THE LONGEST RIVER IN THE WORLD, WHAT RIVER IS SHE SAILING ON?

9 WHICH 555-FOOT-TALL US MONUMENT SHAPED LIKE AN OBELISK WAS OPENED TO THE PUBLIC IN 1888?

10 THOMAS JEFFERSON IS FEATURED ON WHAT CURRENT US COIN?

11 EGYPT IS LOCATED MOSTLY WITHIN WHICH GIANT DESERT?
A. GOBI   B. MOJAVE   C. SAHARA

12 WHICH OF THESE IS A PROVINCE IN CANADA?
A. MANITOBA   B. BROITOBA   C. DUDEITOBA

SECOND GRADE

1

TRUE OR FALSE? SOME PARTS OF CANADA ARE FARTHER SOUTH THAN PARTS OF THE US.

2

WHICH OF THE FOLLOWING CITIES ARE CLOSEST IN DISTANCE?
A. BOSTON, MA, AND SAN DIEGO, CA
B. LAS VEGAS, NV, AND BALTIMORE, MD
C. AUSTIN, TX, AND MINNEAPOLIS, MN

3

FILL IN THE BLANK FROM THE DECLARATION OF INDEPENDENCE: "WE HOLD THESE _____ TO BE SELF-EVIDENT."

4

WHAT IS THE OFFICIAL NAME OF THE US NATIONAL ANTHEM?
A. "THE STAR-SPANGLED BANNER"
B. "OH, SAY CAN YOU SEE"
C. "AMERICA THE BEAUTIFUL"

5

THE PYRAMIDS OF GIZA ARE LOCATED IN WHAT MODERN-DAY COUNTRY?

6

THE YEAR 1912 WAS IN WHAT CENTURY?
 A. 18TH CENTURY   B. 19TH CENTURY   C. 20TH CENTURY

7

"GIVE ME YOUR TIRED, YOUR POOR, YOUR HUDDLED MASSES YEARNING TO BREATHE FREE" IS A QUOTE FROM A POEM LOCATED AT THE BASE OF WHAT US NATIONAL MONUMENT?

8

WHAT IS THE TOTAL NUMBER OF SHIPS THAT CHRISTOPHER COLUMBUS SET SAIL WITH ON HIS FIRST VOYAGE TO THE NEW WORLD IN 1492?

9

BRAZIL HAS OVER 4,500 MILES OF COASTLINE ALONG WHICH OCEAN?

10

IN TERMS OF LAND AREA, WHICH OF THE SEVEN CONTINENTS IS THE SECOND SMALLEST?

11

WHEN IT COMES TO LAWMAKING AND BILLS, WHAT'S THE ROLE OF THE PRESIDENT?
 A. HE INTRODUCES THE BILL.
 B. HE SIGNS THE BILL.
 C. HE GOES DUTCH ON THE BILL.

12

THE GREAT BARRIER REEF IS LOCATED CLOSEST TO THE COAST OF WHAT CONTINENT?

THIRD GRADE

1 IN GREEK MYTHOLOGY, THE GODDESS OF WISDOM, ATHENA, WAS THE DAUGHTER OF WHICH GOD?

2 WHICH OF THESE RIVERS LIES ENTIRELY WITHIN THE US?
A. COLORADO RIVER
B. MISSISSIPPI RIVER
C. YUKON RIVER

3 IN 1979, WHO BECAME THE FIRST WOMAN TO BE FEATURED ON US CURRENCY?

4 WHICH OF THE SEVEN CONTINENTS WAS THE LAST TO BE DISCOVERED?

5 THE US TREASURY BUILDING IS PICTURED ON THE BACK OF WHAT DENOMINATION OF CURRENCY?

6 THE FLAG OF WHAT US STATE FEATURES THE CONSTELLATION KNOWN AS THE BIG DIPPER?

7 THE LAND THAT IS NOW CALLED NEW YORK CITY WAS FIRST COLONIZED BY SETTLERS FROM WHAT COUNTRY?

8

NAMED AFTER ITS FRENCH CREATOR, WHAT SYSTEM OF READING AND WRITING FOR THE BLIND CONSISTS OF OVER SIXTY CHARACTERS MADE UP OF RAISED DOTS?

9

WHICH OF THE FOLLOWING MACHINES WAS PATENTED BY THOMAS EDISON IN THE 1870s?
A. SEWING MACHINE   B. PHONOGRAPH   C. RADIO

10

GREEK PHILOSOPHER ARISTOTLE BELIEVED THAT EVERYTHING WAS MADE UP OF FOUR ELEMENTS. AIR, WATER, AND EARTH WERE THREE OF THOSE ELEMENTS. WHAT WAS THE FOURTH?

11

THE YELLOW AND THE YANGTZE ARE THE TWO LONGEST RIVERS IN WHAT COUNTRY?

12

IN WHAT DECADE DID "THE STAR-SPANGLED BANNER" OFFICIALLY BECOME THE NATIONAL ANTHEM OF THE UNITED STATES THROUGH AN ACT OF CONGRESS?
A. 1790s   B. 1860s   C. 1930s

FOURTH GRADE

1

AMIRA BOUGHT POSTCARDS FOR SAYA AS SHE TRAVELED DIRECTLY FROM FLORIDA TO ARIZONA. ACCORDING TO THE CITIES ON THE CARDS, WHICH ONE DID SHE BUY FIRST?

A. "GREETINGS FROM AUSTIN"
B. "HELLO FROM PHOENIX"
C. "I LOVE NEW ORLEANS"

2

NOW A NATIONAL HISTORICAL PARK, WHAT SITE WAS HEADQUARTERS FOR GEORGE WASHINGTON'S ARMY IN THE WINTER OF 1777-78?

3

WHICH BRANCH OF THE FEDERAL GOVERNMENT MAKES LAWS?

A. LEGISLATIVE
B. EXECUTIVE
C. JUDICIAL

4

THE APPALACHIAN MOUNTAINS EXTEND FOR ALMOST 2,000 MILES FROM CANADA AND END IN WHAT SOUTHERN US STATE?

5 WHAT US STATE WAS NAMED FOR QUEEN HENRIETTA MARIA, THE WIFE OF KING CHARLES I OF ENGLAND?

6 WHEN ADDRESSING A LETTER TO SOMEONE IN MAINE, WHAT TWO-LETTER US POSTAL ABBREVIATION SHOULD YOU USE?

7 IN WHICH CENTURY WAS THE FIRST AUTOMOBILE INVENTED?
A. 18TH CENTURY   B. 19TH CENTURY   C. 20TH CENTURY

8 KNOWN AS THE "FATHER OF THE NATIONAL PARKS," WHAT AMERICAN NATURALIST FOUNDED AND BECAME THE FIRST PRESIDENT OF THE SIERRA CLUB IN 1892?

9 ALTHOUGH HE BECAME KING OF ENGLAND, WILLIAM THE CONQUEROR WAS BORN IN WHAT MODERN-DAY COUNTRY?

10 THE OFFICIAL FLAG OF WHAT US STATE PICTURES A BEAVER ON ONE SIDE AND THE STATE SEAL ON THE OTHER?

11 THE WATERFALLS KNOWN AS NIAGARA FALLS SERVE AS THE BORDER BETWEEN NEW YORK AND WHAT CANADIAN PROVINCE?

12 ASSUMING THERE ARE NO VACANCIES, WHAT IS THE TOTAL NUMBER OF REPRESENTATIVES IN THE US HOUSE OF REPRESENTATIVES FROM THE FIFTY US STATES?

FIFTH GRADE

1 THE BATTLE OF WATERLOO, AT WHICH NAPOLEON WAS DEFEATED, WAS FOUGHT IN WHAT COUNTRY?

2 IN 1762, CATHERINE THE GREAT SUCCEEDED HER HUSBAND PETER III TO BECOME EMPRESS OF WHAT COUNTRY?

3 WHAT IS THE MINIMUM NUMBER OF ELECTORAL COLLEGE VOTES A CANDIDATE MUST RECEIVE TO WIN A US PRESIDENTIAL ELECTION?

4 WHAT KING MARRIED ANNE BOLEYN IN 1533 AND DECLARED HIMSELF HEAD OF THE CHURCH OF ENGLAND?

5 WHAT BRIDGE, COMPLETED IN 1964, IS THE LONGEST SUSPENSION BRIDGE IN NORTH AMERICA?

6 CLARA BARTON, A PIONEERING NURSE AND TEACHER, HELPED ORGANIZE AND BECAME THE FIRST PRESIDENT OF WHICH ORGANIZATION IN 1881?

7

WASHINGTON CROSSED THE DELAWARE RIVER ON CHRISTMAS NIGHT 1776 TO ATTACK HESSIAN FORCES IN WHAT US CITY?

8

BORN ARAMINTA ROSS, WHAT IS THE MORE COMMONLY KNOWN NAME OF THE WOMAN WHO HELPED PEOPLE USE THE UNDERGROUND RAILROAD?

9

COMPLETED IN 1883 AND DESIGNED BY JOHN ROEBLING, WHAT WAS THE FIRST SUSPENSION BRIDGE IN THE US TO USE STEEL FOR ITS CABLE WIRE?

10

CONGRESS ESTABLISHED A NATIONAL MONUMENT HONORING WHAT NINETEENTH-CENTURY AFRICAN-AMERICAN INVENTOR WHO DEVELOPED OVER THREE HUNDRED USES FOR PEANUTS AND SWEET POTATOES?

11

WHAT BUILDING IS PICTURED ON THE BACK OF A US $100 BILL?

12

MANFRED VON RICHTHOFEN WAS A GERMAN AVIATOR WHO WAS NICKNAMED THE "RED BARON" AND FAMOUSLY FOUGHT IN WHAT WAR?

LET'S
PLAY!

FIRST GRADE

1 The White House is located on what avenue in Washington, DC?

2 What city is the capital of Mexico?

SECOND GRADE

3 What US state's postal abbreviation is "MI"?

4 How many US states share a border with another state?

5 Excluding Greenland, what is the third-largest country in North America in terms of area?

THIRD GRADE

6 President Lyndon B. Johnson was born in what state?

7 Paul Revere made his famous midnight ride through Massachusetts on April 18 of what year?

8 What Greek god of the sea was brother to Zeus and Hades?

FOURTH GRADE

9 The SS *Ancon* became the first ship to officially pass through what canal on August 15, 1914?

10 What is the only US state that borders only one other US state?

11 The Suez Canal, completed in the 1800s, connects the Mediterranean Sea with what other sea?

FIFTH GRADE

12 The "Rough Riders" was the name given to the first United States volunteer cavalry, whose members included what future US president?

13 Easter Island is closest in distance to which of the seven continents?

14 William Seward spearheaded the purchase of what US state in 1867, in a transaction that came to be known as "Seward's Folly"?

BONUS

What amendment to the US Constitution grants women the right to vote in federal elections?

FIRST GRADE

1 WHAT MASSIVE RELATIVE OF THE DEER KNOWN FOR ITS ANTLERS IS THE STATE ANIMAL OF MAINE?

2 WHAT MONTH, DATE, AND YEAR ARE LISTED AT THE TOP OF THE DECLARATION OF INDEPENDENCE?

SECOND GRADE

3 WHAT NINETEENTH-CENTURY MAIL SERVICE IN THE US CARRIED LETTERS OVER 2,000 MILES IN TEN DAYS BY HORSEBACK?

4 WHAT ANCIENT CIVILIZATION HAD RULERS KNOWN AS PHARAOHS?
   A. EGYPTIANS   B. GREEKS   C. ROMANS

5 PLYMOUTH ROCK, THE SITE WHERE THE PILGRIMS LANDED IN 1620, IS LOCATED IN WHAT US STATE?
   A. VIRGINIA   B. MASSACHUSETTS   C. NEW HAMPSHIRE

THIRD GRADE

6 "EUREKA" IS THE MOTTO OF WHAT US STATE?

7 WHICH OF THE FOLLOWING OFFICEHOLDERS IS TYPICALLY ELECTED TO THE SHORTEST TERM?
   A. US PRESIDENT   B. US REPRESENTATIVE   C. US SENATOR

8 NAMED FOR THE INVENTOR WHO CREATED IT IN THE 1830s, WHAT CODE BREAKS DOWN THE ALPHABET INTO DOTS AND DASHES FOR SENDING MESSAGES?

FOURTH GRADE

9 MEANING "EVER UPWARD," "EXCELSIOR" IS THE OFFICIAL MOTTO FOR WHAT US STATE?

10 THE SERENGETI IS A GEOGRAPHICAL REGION IN AFRICA THAT IS HOME TO MANY WILD ANIMALS, SUCH AS WILDEBEESTS AND GAZELLES. THE SERENGETI IS LOCATED IN KENYA AND WHAT OTHER COUNTRY?

11 THE GANGES RIVER ORIGINATES IN THE HIMALAYAS, FLOWS THROUGH INDIA AND BANGLADESH, AND EMPTIES INTO WHICH BAY THAT IS PART OF THE INDIAN OCEAN?

FIFTH GRADE

12 WHAT MOUNTAIN RANGE INCLUDES MOUNT RAINIER AND MOUNT ST. HELENS?

13 WHAT CIVIL WAR GENERAL LED HIS TROOPS IN A FAMOUS "MARCH TO THE SEA" ACROSS GEORGIA IN 1864?

14 ONE OF THE SEVEN WONDERS OF THE ANCIENT WORLD, THE TEMPLE OF ARTEMIS WAS LOCATED AT EPHESUS, WHICH IS NOW PART OF WHAT COUNTRY?

BONUS

WHAT WAS THE FIRST US STATE TO ALLOW WOMEN THE RIGHT TO VOTE?

FIRST GRADE

1 What US president is featured on the $1 bill?

2 What animal is featured on the Great Seal of the United States?

SECOND GRADE

3 Which of the following is the state bird for the greatest number of US states?

    a. cardinal
    b. robin
    c. turkey

4 On March 4, 1789, the First United States Congress was called to order in what city?

5 If Quinne is visiting the country of Uganda, she can be found on which continent?

THIRD GRADE

6 Which of the following monuments is tallest?

    a. Gateway Arch
    b. Statue of Liberty
    c. Washington Monument

7 The blue-tiled Ishtar Gate was the entrance to what ancient city that was also the home of the famous Hanging Gardens?

8 The first six US presidents all came from either Virginia or what other US state?

    a. Massachusetts
    b. New York
    c. Pennsylvania

FOURTH GRADE

9 The Klondike gold rush of the 1890s primarily took place in what Canadian territory?

10 The USS *Constitution*, which is still afloat near Boston, Massachusetts, got the nickname "Old Ironsides" during a battle in what war?

11 In 1789, an angry mob set off a revolution by storming a prison called the Bastille in what city?

FIFTH GRADE

12 After losing the Battle of Waterloo, Napoleon Bonaparte was exiled to what island in 1815?

13 If Wyoming had one member of the US House of Representatives, how many electoral votes would it have?

14 The original Bill of Rights is located in what building found in Washington, DC?

BONUS

Who was the last Habsburg emperor of the Austro-Hungarian Empire?

FIRST GRADE

1 If Chloe is speaking Hungarian, she is speaking the official language of what country that has Budapest as its capital?

2 TRUE OR FALSE? If Colin visits Madrid, Spain, then he'll be standing on the continent of Europe.

SECOND GRADE

3 What amendment to the US Constitution guarantees freedom of speech and the press?

4 The pua aloalo is the official flower of what US state?

5 In the US Declaration of Independence, what six words immediately follow the phrase "We hold these truths to be self-evident"?

THIRD GRADE

6 UNICEF and UNESCO are branches of what international organization?

7 The deepest point in the Atlantic Ocean reaches approximately how many feet below sea level?
a. 8,000 feet
b. 28,000 feet
c. 48,000 feet

8 TRUE OR FALSE? The Spanish alphabet has more letters than the English alphabet.

FOURTH GRADE

9 In what war did American general Benedict Arnold shift his allegiance from the US to the British?

10 Which amendment in the US Bill of Rights prohibits unreasonable search and seizure without a warrant?

11 Benjamin Franklin signed the Declaration of Independence as a representative from which new state?

FIFTH GRADE

12 In order to be president of the United States, a person must be at least how many years of age?

13 After serving as prime minister of Great Britain for much of World War II, Winston Churchill lost the election of 1945. What man then became prime minister?

14 If a US president is impeached and all one hundred senators are voting, how many votes are needed to remove them from office?

BONUS

During the Civil War, how many states seceded from the Union?

FIRST GRADE

1 The west coast of Mexico borders which ocean?

2 What Washington, DC, memorial, dedicated in 1922, is named in honor of the sixteenth US president?

SECOND GRADE

3 What US state known for its cheese has the dairy cow as its state animal?

4 The terms "status quo," "bona fide," and "per capita" are all taken from what ancient language?

5 The ancient Inca Empire bordered which ocean?

THIRD GRADE

6 Abraham Lincoln was the first man to be elected US president as a member of which political party?

7 In the US army, which of the following officer classes ranks the highest?

    a. captain
    b. lieutenant
    c. major

8 Who was the first US vice president to be elected US president?

FOURTH GRADE

9 With a tenure lasting from 1801 to 1835, who was the longest-serving chief justice in the history of the US Supreme Court?

10 What US state takes its name from the Spanish for "mountain"?

11 Renaissance artist and inventor Leonardo da Vinci was born in 1452 in what modern-day country?

FIFTH GRADE

12 Nicknamed "Old Fuss and Feathers," Winfield Scott was a US army general who lost the US presidential election of 1852 to what man?

13 What was the name of the first satellite successfully launched into space in 1957?

14 The House of Burgesses was the first elective assembly of the thirteen original colonies. What colony was it in?

BONUS

On August 3, 1492, Christopher Columbus's first voyage to the Americas departed from what Spanish port?

FIRST GRADE

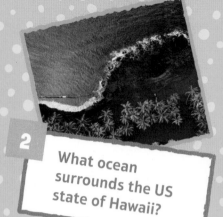

1 In the US, the Independence Day national holiday occurs in which of the four seasons?

2 What ocean surrounds the US state of Hawaii?

SECOND GRADE

3 What is the last country the Colorado River flows through before it reaches the Gulf of California?

4 Four US states have names that begin and end with the same letter. Alabama, Alaska, and Arizona are three. What is the fourth?

5 Until 1954, what US federal holiday celebrated in November was known as Armistice Day?

THIRD GRADE

6 The original Pony Express was a rapid postal system in the US by which mail was delivered by riders on horseback. In what century did it operate?

7 By definition, the Dewey Decimal System is used to organize which of the following?
a. people
b. books
c. planets

8 Over 14,000 feet high, Mount Rainier is a volcanic mountain peak in what US state?

FOURTH GRADE

9 Immediately before joining the Union in 1820, Maine was part of which other US state?

10 Born in 1822, what French chemist, known for his work in preventing bacteria in milk, also pioneered a vaccine for rabies?

11 At the time of the French Revolution, the "First Estate" referred to which of the following?
   a. the common people
   b. the clergy
   c. the nobility

FIFTH GRADE

12 What president renamed the official US presidential retreat "Camp David" after his grandson?

13 The 1848 Treaty of Guadalupe Hidalgo ended the war between the US and what other country?

14 The tiny nation of San Marino is completely surrounded by what other European country?

BONUS

Who was the first man to be US president when the United States had fifty states?

FIRST GRADE

1 WHAT MAN WAS THE SECOND PRESIDENT OF THE UNITED STATES?

2 IN 1620, WHAT SHIP SAILED FROM ENGLAND TO A SITE IN PRESENT-DAY MASSACHUSETTS?

SECOND GRADE

3 FAMOUS FOR PATENTING 1,093 INVENTIONS, WHAT AMERICAN INVENTOR WAS KNOWN AS "THE WIZARD OF MENLO PARK"?

4 WHAT IS THE ONLY US STATE THAT HAS TERRITORY ABOVE THE ARCTIC CIRCLE?

5 WHAT IS THE OFFICIAL FLOWER OF THE UNITED STATES?

THIRD GRADE

6 TRUE OR FALSE? THE ISLAND OF BARBADOS IS AN INDEPENDENT COUNTRY.

7 QUITO IS THE CAPITAL OF WHAT SOUTH AMERICAN COUNTRY?

8 WHO WAS THE YOUNGEST PERSON TO BE ELECTED PRESIDENT OF

FOURTH GRADE

9 WHAT US STATE IS HOME TO THE FIRST NATIONAL MONUMENT AND THE FIRST NATIONAL PARK?

10 HERBERT HOOVER, WHO WAS IN OFFICE DURING A FAMOUS STOCK MARKET CRASH, WAS ELECTED US PRESIDENT IN WHAT DECADE?

11 IN 1917, LENIN BECAME THE LEADER OF RUSSIA. WHAT WAS HIS FIRST NAME?

FIFTH GRADE

12 BORN IN UTAH IN 1906, WHAT AMERICAN INVENTOR WAS THE FIRST PERSON TO TRANSMIT A TELEVISION IMAGE IN 1927?

13 WHAT US VICE PRESIDENT RESIGNED IN 1832 AND WENT ON TO BECOME A SENATOR FROM SOUTH CAROLINA?

14 A PEOPLE OF POLYNESIAN ORIGIN, THE MĀORI ARE NATIVE INHABITANTS OF WHAT COUNTRY LOCATED IN THE SOUTHERN HEMISPHERE?

BONUS

WHAT IS THE ONLY COUNTRY IN THE WORLD WHOSE OFFICIAL NATIONAL FLAG

FIRST GRADE

1 Before they declared their independence in 1776, the thirteen original American colonies belonged to what country?

SECOND GRADE

3 Mexico's Independence Day takes place on the sixteenth of what month?

THIRD GRADE

6 The land comprising the modern state of Florida was purchased from what country in 1819?

7 What American founding father is credited with saying "Early to bed and early to rise makes a man healthy, wealthy, and wise"?

2 What national monument in New York Harbor features a statue of a woman that's 151 feet tall when measured from her feet to the top of her torch?

4 Which of the following US coins has an image of the president who served in office most recently?

    a. nickel

    b. penny

    c. quarter

5 Colorado is nicknamed "the Centennial State" because it became a US state in what year?

8 Awarded to US soldiers, the Purple Heart features the image of which US president?

    a. George Washington

    b. Herbert Hoover

    c. Richard Nixon

FOURTH GRADE

9 What US state is divided into sixty-four parishes rather than counties?

10 In 1933, what US president said in his first inaugural address, "The only thing we have to fear is fear itself"?

11 Which branch of Congress must approve the nomination of a US Supreme Court justice?

FIFTH GRADE

12 The United Nations is an international organization that supports world peace. In what year did the United States officially join the United Nations?

13 What is the only US state that was an independent kingdom with its own monarchy before entering the union?

14 Who was the first woman to be both the wife and mother of a US president?

BONUS

The Volga River is the longest river in what country?

FIRST GRADE

1 **TRUE OR FALSE?** The Pilgrims arrived at Plymouth Rock in 1620 with three ships, the *Niña*, the *Pinta*, and the *Santa Maria*.

2 Two countries border the Great Lakes. The United States is one of them. What is the other?

SECOND GRADE

5 In what year will the United States celebrate its tricentennial?

4 How many chief justices serve on the US Supreme Court?

3 What building in Washington, DC, serves as the official meeting place for the US Congress?

7 **TRUE OR FALSE?** A US presidential veto cannot be overridden.

6 What is the capital of the US state of Kentucky?

THIRD GRADE

8 In the US presidential oath of office, the president swears to "preserve, protect and defend" what document?

FOURTH GRADE

9 Who was US president immediately before Abraham Lincoln?

10 The secretary of education is a member of the Cabinet, which is part of what branch of the US government?

11 The majority of the Outer Banks, a 175-mile stretch of sandy barrier islands, are located in what US state?

FIFTH GRADE

12 Shays' Rebellion, which made lawmakers realize they needed a stronger central government, originated in what US state in the 1780s?

13 During World War I, what British luxury ocean liner was torpedoed and sunk by a German submarine on May 7, 1915?

14 Who was president of the US during the Mexican-American War?

BONUS What 1803 US Supreme Court case established the precedent of judicial review?

FIRST GRADE

1 What is the official name for the federal holiday celebrated on July 4?

    a. Flag Day
    b. Independence Day
    c. Patriot Day

2 What country's flag was the first to be placed on the moon?

SECOND GRADE

3 The image of what US president is featured on the current US $5 bill?

4 The United States borders how many bodies of water?

5 Nefertiti was a fourteenth-century BC queen of what ancient civilization?

THIRD GRADE

6 The Tasman Sea is part of what ocean?

7 What US president commissioned the nineteenth-century cross-country expedition led by explorers Meriwether Lewis and William Clark?

8 Which of the following ancient civilizations came first?

    a. Incas
    b. Vikings
    c. Spartans

FOURTH GRADE

9 The metric system originated in the 1790s in what country?

10 The Nobel Prize in chemistry is given out annually in what country?

11 What US president founded and designed the layout of the University of Virginia?

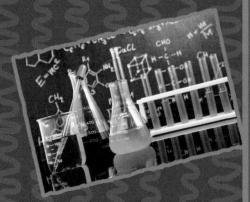

FIFTH GRADE

12 What Roman general born in the second-century BC is credited with saying, "I came, I saw, I conquered"?

13 At the beginning of the US Civil War, what state was the first to officially secede from the Union?

14 Who was the only US president to have earned a PhD before taking office?

BONUS

What Spanish explorer conquered Peru in the 1530s and also became its governor?

FIRST GRADE

1 US presidential elections always occur on what day of the week?

2 What is the only US state whose name starts with two vowels?

SECOND GRADE

3 **TRUE OR FALSE?** Tallahassee, Florida, is the southernmost US state capital.

4 What ocean surrounds the North Pole?

5 The Rio Grande empties into what body of water?

THIRD GRADE

6 During the Ice Age, North America was connected to which continent via a land bridge that no longer exists?

7 **TRUE OR FALSE?** US president Benjamin Harrison was the son of US president William Henry Harrison.

8 In Greek mythology, what woman released all the evils into the world after looking into a box she was told never to open?

FOURTH GRADE

9 Which of these states was most recently admitted to the Union, in 1912?
  a. Arizona
  b. Texas
  c. California

10 In Roman mythology, what creatures of the woodland were half man and half goat?

11 During what war did President Harry Truman fire General Douglas MacArthur for insubordination?

FIFTH GRADE

12 What candidate received a majority of the popular vote in the US presidential election of 2016 but did not become president?

13 Apollo 17 was the last mission to land a man on the moon. In what year did it take place?

14 During the War of 1812, Tecumseh was a Native American who sided with the British. Tecumseh was the leader of what tribe?

BONUS

In one of the most important elections in US history, Abraham Lincoln was elected president in 1860. Who was his vice president?

FIRST GRADE

1. TRUE OR FALSE? FOR AS LONG AS THEY HAVE BEEN MINTED, US PENNIES HAVE BEEN 99.99 PERCENT COPPER.

2. THE SUGAR MAPLE IS THE OFFICIAL TREE FOR WHAT US STATE THAT ENTERED THE UNION IN 1791?

SECOND GRADE

3. TRUE OR FALSE? THE LIBERTY BELL IN PHILADELPHIA CRACKED IN 1776 AND WAS NEVER RUNG AGAIN.

4. EXCLUDING POLAR REGIONS, WHAT IS THE LARGEST DESERT IN THE WORLD IN TERMS OF AREA?

5. WHAT INVENTOR RECEIVED THE FIRST PATENT FOR THE TELEPHONE IN 1876 AT THE AGE OF TWENTY-NINE?

THIRD GRADE

6. WHICH OF THESE US STATES WAS ONE OF THE ORIGINAL THIRTEEN COLONIES?
   A. OHIO   B. ALABAMA   C. NORTH CAROLINA

7. WHAT MONTH IS NAMED FOR THE ROMAN GOD OF WAR?

8. "THE PELICAN STATE" IS THE OFFICIAL NICKNAME OF WHAT US STATE?

FOURTH GRADE

9 WHAT MAN WAS THE US SECRETARY OF WAR AND PROVISIONAL GOVERNOR OF CUBA BEFORE BEING ELECTED PRESIDENT IN 1908?

10 WHAT US STATE CAPITAL IS THE HIGHEST IN ELEVATION?

11 LOCATED IN THE CITY OF SALEM, MAHONIA HALL IS THE NAME OF THE OFFICIAL GOVERNOR'S RESIDENCE IN WHICH US STATE?

FIFTH GRADE

12 THE LOUISIANA PURCHASE WAS A TRANSACTION BETWEEN THE UNITED STATES AND WHAT OTHER COUNTRY?

13 IN 1931, FAMED GANGSTER AL CAPONE WAS CONVICTED OF WHAT FEDERAL CRIME?

14 KABUKI IS A TRADITIONAL TYPE OF THEATER THAT ORIGINATES IN WHAT COUNTRY?

BONUS

THE HIGHEST SUSPENSION BRIDGE IN THE UNITED STATES SPANS THE ROYAL GORGE IN WHAT STATE?

FIRST GRADE

1 **TRUE OR FALSE? New Jersey was one of the original thirteen colonies.**

2 How many of the seven continents have two-word names?

SECOND GRADE

5 King Tut was a ruler of what ancient civilization?

3 **TRUE OR FALSE? The first official flag of the United States had fifty stars.**

4 Mount Olympus, which is over 9,000 feet tall, is the highest mountain in what country?

THIRD GRADE

7 Located in Washington, DC, the Thomas Jefferson Building is part of what US government complex that contains twenty public reading rooms?

6 In the US federal government, what member of the executive branch appoints federal judges?

    a. the president
    b. the attorney general
    c. the chief justice of the Supreme Court

8 Recorded in Death Valley, California, the highest temperature in US history was which of the following?

    a. 134 degrees F
    b. 154 degrees F
    c. 174 degrees F

FOURTH GRADE

9 Which of these men led the American army to victory in the Battle of New Orleans during the War of 1812?

    a. Ulysses S. Grant
    b. Alexander Hamilton
    c. Andrew Jackson

FIFTH GRADE

10 Explorer Sir Walter Raleigh, known for his attempts to colonize Roanoke Island in modern-day North Carolina, was knighted by what British monarch?

11 Phnom Penh is the capital city of what Asian country?

    a. Cambodia
    b. Indonesia
    c. Thailand

12 In 1955, who famously fought for civil rights by refusing to give up her seat on a Montgomery, Alabama, bus?

13 Who was queen of England when the English defeated the Spanish Armada in 1588?

14 Once home to US soldiers who would protect travelers on the Oregon Trail, Fort Laramie is located in what present-day state?

BONUS

The text of the Twentieth Amendment to the US Constitution states that Congress shall meet at least once a year and such meeting shall be on what date?

FIRST GRADE

1 Seventeenth-century composer Antonio Vivaldi, famous for *The Four Seasons* concertos, was born in what modern-day country?

2 If November 1 falls on a Monday, the US holiday of Thanksgiving is celebrated on what date?

SECOND GRADE

5 In 1814, what US first lady saved the portrait of George Washington and, perhaps, the Declaration of Independence from a fire at the White House?

3 The majority of Florida lies on what type of landform?
a. isthmus
b. peninsula
c. atoll

4 The majority of US coins are made in which of the following places?
a. the White House
b. the US Mint
c. the Library of Congress

THIRD GRADE

6 What US president gave a speech in 1863 in which he stated "that government of the people, by the people, for the people, shall not perish from the earth?"

7 What US state won its independence from Mexico in 1835 but had to wait ten years before the US would annex it?

8 Which man featured on the face of Mount Rushmore served as US president most recently?

FOURTH GRADE

9 How many other US states border Tennessee?

10 What country was the birthplace of Genghis Khan?

11 In the 1930s, what military reservation in Kentucky became the designated location for the bulk of America's gold reserve?

FIFTH GRADE

12 In 1921, what man who later became known for his role in the Teapot Dome scandal became the first US president to ride in an automobile to his inauguration?

13 What was the first European country to recognize the United States as an independent nation?

14 Between 1455 and 1485, the War of the Roses took place in what country?

BONUS

Which of the original thirteen colonies had the greatest number of representatives sign the Declaration of Independence?

FIRST GRADE

1 The geyser Old Faithful erupts on average every ninety minutes in what US national park?

2 What country has red-coated policemen who are nicknamed "Mounties"?

SECOND GRADE

3 TRUE OR FALSE? The US Supreme Court is the highest court in the United States.

4 What is the only US state whose name begins with the letter "D"?

5 The ancient Olympic Games originated during the eighth century BC in what modern-day country?
   a. Egypt
   b. Greece
   c. Italy

THIRD GRADE

6 After New York City and Los Angeles, what is the third most populated city in the US?

7 How many months of the current year contain no US federal holidays?
   a. 2
   b. 4
   c. 6

8 There are five branches of the United States armed forces. The marines, air force, army, and navy are four. What is the fifth?

FOURTH GRADE

9 What former first lady was appointed by President Harry Truman as a delegate to the United Nations?

10 What is the three-word radio call sign used by any US air force aircraft that carries the US president?

11 General George Washington defeated the British at the Battle of Yorktown in 1781 with help from the navy of what European country?

FIFTH GRADE

12 Who was US president when the Statue of Liberty was dedicated in 1886?

13 Designated as a world heritage site, Cappadocia is a centuries-old complex of caves carved into ancient volcanic rock located in what country?

14 Before the Revolution of 1917, the Romanovs were the monarchs of what country?

BONUS

There are only two countries in the world with a square national flag. The Vatican is one. What is the other?

FIRST GRADE

1 What city has been the capital of the United States for over two hundred years?

2 Christopher Columbus's voyages to America were funded by the king and queen of what country?

SECOND GRADE

3 What US state is home to a chain of islands known as the "Keys"?

4 Occupying over 2 million square feet, the Metropolitan Museum of Art is located in what US city?

5 Lewis and Clark's famous 1804 expedition ended on the shore of which ocean?

THIRD GRADE

6 Officially opened on February 2, 1913, and home to Vanderbilt Hall, Grand Central Terminal is located in what US city?

7 From 1910 to 1940, Angel Island served as the port of entry into the US for thousands of Asian immigrants. Angel Island is a part of what US state?

8 Designed and lived in by US president Thomas Jefferson, what estate, over two hundred years old, is located in Virginia?

FOURTH GRADE

9 What man was both the president of Mexico and the commanding general of the Mexican army during the siege of the Alamo in the 1830s?

10 Born in 1820, what British nurse was nicknamed "the Lady with the Lamp" because she often worked through the night to bring aid to wounded soldiers?

11 Authorized by Thomas Jefferson, the Cumberland Road ultimately followed which of the following routes?
   a. Georgia to Oklahoma
   b. Maryland to Illinois
   c. New York to Michigan

FIFTH GRADE

12 The peace treaty ending the War of 1812 was signed in what year?

13 What river forms the boundary between the US states of South Carolina and Georgia?

14 In Greek mythology, what brother of Zeus was the god of the underworld?

BONUS

On February 18, 1861, Jefferson Davis was sworn in as president of the Confederacy in what present-day US state?

FIRST GRADE

1 IF MIA IS VISITING THE NATION OF THAILAND, WHAT CONTINENT IS SHE ON?

2 HOW MANY STRIPES ARE ON THE CURRENT US FLAG?

SECOND GRADE

3 IN THE UNITED STATES, THE HOLIDAY KNOWN AS GROUNDHOG DAY IS TRADITIONALLY OBSERVED IN WHAT MONTH?
A. FEBRUARY   B. AUGUST   C. NOVEMBER

4 OLYMPIC NATIONAL PARK IS LOCATED IN WHAT US STATE?

5 WHICH OF THE FOLLOWING US STATES BORDERS BOTH SOUTH DAKOTA AND ILLINOIS?
A. IOWA   B. MINNESOTA   C. WISCONSIN

THIRD GRADE

6 WHAT COUNTRY'S FLAG FEATURES AN EAGLE STANDING ON A CACTUS AND HOLDING A SNAKE IN ITS BEAK?

7 WHAT STATE BORDERS NORTH DAKOTA TO THE WEST?

8 WHAT US NAVAL BASE THAT IS THE HEADQUARTERS OF THE PACIFIC FLEET WAS ATTACKED BY JAPAN ON DECEMBER 7, 1941?

FOURTH GRADE

9 WHO WAS US PRESIDENT WHEN THE NORTH ATLANTIC TREATY ORGANIZATION, COMMONLY KNOWN AS NATO, WAS FORMED?

10 CREATED IN 1787, THE NORTHWEST TERRITORY INCLUDED LAND THAT LATER BECAME WHICH OF THE FOLLOWING US STATES?

    A. OREGON B. OKLAHOMA C. OHIO

11 TRUE OR FALSE? BENJAMIN FRANKLIN WAS SECRETARY OF STATE FOR US PRESIDENT GEORGE WASHINGTON.

FIFTH GRADE

12 THE BANTU GROUP OF LANGUAGES ARE SPOKEN PRIMARILY ON WHICH CONTINENT?

13 HUDSON BAY AND THE HUDSON RIVER ARE NAMED FOR AN ENGLISH EXPLORER WHO HAD WHAT FIRST NAME?

14 WHAT LAWYER WHO ARGUED BEFORE THE US SUPREME COURT IN *BROWN V. BOARD OF EDUCATION OF TOPEKA* LATER BECAME A SUPREME COURT JUSTICE HIMSELF?

BONUS

WHAT DOCUMENT THAT PRECEDED THE CONSTITUTION GAVE CONGRESS THE AUTHORITY TO GOVERN THE UNITED STATES BETWEEN 1781 AND 1789?

FIRST GRADE

1 Dedicated in 1886, what New York Harbor monument features a statue holding a torch in her right hand?

2 The Grand Canyon is located in what US state?

SECOND GRADE

3 TRUE OR FALSE? The Tropic of Capricorn is south of the equator.

4 TRUE OR FALSE? If Jamir is standing on the east coast of Asia, he can dive into the Pacific Ocean.

5 With an official elevation of 5,280 feet, what US city of around 700,000 people is known as the "Mile High City"?

THIRD GRADE

6 Idaho is bordered by how many states?

7 In 1791, what became the fourteenth US state to join the Union?

8 What river forms the border between Arizona and California?

FOURTH GRADE

9 What US president had the campaign slogan "I Like Ike"?

10 The Berlin Wall once separated East Berlin from West Berlin. Construction of the wall began in what decade?

11 In 1933, what US president began giving a series of speeches on the radio known as "fireside chats"?

FIFTH GRADE

12 Located in Maryland, the US presidential retreat known as Camp David is run by which branch of the US armed forces?

13 Helping to establish the spice trade, Vasco da Gama's expedition around the Cape of Good Hope eventually reached what country in May 1498?

14 What name did abolitionist Isabella Baumfree take when she became a traveling preacher and delivered the speech "Ain't I a Woman"?

BONUS

In what year did the British passenger ship *Titanic* sink on its maiden voyage across the Atlantic?

ANSWER KEY

PAGES 8-9:
FIRST GRADE

1. "liberty and justice for all"
2. Colorado
3. Indian Ocean
4. false
5. Atlantic
6. Thanksgiving
7. John Hancock
8. Nile River
9. Washington Monument
10. nickel
11. c
12. a

PAGES 10-11:
SECOND GRADE

1. true
2. c
3. truths
4. a
5. Egypt
6. c
7. Statue of Liberty
8. 3
9. Atlantic
10. Europe
11. b
12. Australia

PAGES 12-13:
THIRD GRADE

1. Zeus
2. b
3. Susan B. Anthony
4. Antarctica
5. $10 bill
6. Alaska
7. the Netherlands
8. braille
9. b
10. fire
11. China
12. c

PAGES 14-15:
FOURTH GRADE

1. c
2. Valley Forge, Pennsylvania
3. a
4. Alabama
5. Maryland
6. ME
7. b
8. John Muir
9. France
10. Oregon
11. Ontario
12. 435

PAGES 16-17:
FIFTH GRADE

1. Belgium
2. Russia
3. 270
4. Henry VIII
5. Verrazzano (Narrows) Bridge
6. the American Red Cross
7. Trenton, New Jersey
8. Harriet Tubman
9. Brooklyn Bridge
10. George Washington Carver
11. Independence Hall
12. World War I

PAGES 20-21:

1. Pennsylvania Avenue
2. Mexico City
3. Michigan
4. 48
5. Mexico
6. Texas
7. 1775
8. Poseidon
9. Panama Canal
10. Maine
11. Red Sea
12. Theodore Roosevelt
13. South America
14. Alaska
Bonus: Nineteenth Amendment

PAGES 22-23:

1. Moose
2. July 4, 1776
3. Pony Express
4. a
5. b
6. California

7. b
8. Morse (code)
9. New York
10. Tanzania
11. (Bay of) Bengal
12. Cascade Range
13. (William Tecumseh) Sherman
14. Turkey
Bonus: Wyoming

PAGES 24-25:

1. George Washington
2. eagle (also accept: bald eagle)
3. a
4. New York City (also accept: New York)
5. Africa
6. a
7. Babylon
8. a
9. Yukon (Territory)
10. War of 1812
11. Paris
12. St. Helena
13. 3
14. National Archives
Bonus: Charles I

PAGES 26-27:

1. Hungary
2. true
3. First Amendment
4. Hawaii
5. "that all men are created equal"
6. the United Nations
7. b
8. true
9. (US) Revolutionary War
10. Fourth (Amendment)
11. Pennsylvania

12. 35
13. Clement Attlee (also accept: Clem Attlee)
14. 67
Bonus: 11

PAGES 28-29:

1. Pacific
2. Lincoln Memorial
3. Wisconsin
4. Latin
5. Pacific Ocean
6. Republican (also accept: GOP)
7. c
8. John Adams
9. John Marshall
10. Montana
11. Italy
12. Franklin Pierce
13. Sputnik
14. Virginia
Bonus: Palos (de la Frontera)

PAGES 30-31:

1. summer
2. Pacific
3. Mexico
4. Ohio
5. Veterans Day
6. nineteenth (also accept: 1800s)
7. b
8. Washington
9. Massachusetts
10. Louis Pasteur
11. b
12. Dwight D. Eisenhower
13. Mexico
14. Italy
Bonus: Dwight D. Eisenhower

PAGES 32-33:

1. John Adams
2. the *Mayflower*
3. Thomas Edison
4. Alaska
5. rose
6. true
7. Ecuador
8. John F. Kennedy
9. Wyoming
10. 1920s
11. Vladimir
12. Philo Farnsworth
13. John C. Calhoun
14. New Zealand
Bonus: Nepal

PAGES 34-35:

1. England (also accept: Great Britain, Britain, the UK, the United Kingdom)
2. Statue of Liberty
3. September
4. b
5. 1876
6. Spain
7. Benjamin Franklin
8. a
9. Louisiana
10. (Franklin) Roosevelt (also accept: FDR)
11. Senate
12. 1945
13. Hawaii
14. Abigail Adams
Bonus: Russia

PAGES 36-37:

1. false
2. Canada
3. (the US) Capitol (building)

4. 1
5. 2076
6. Frankfort
7. false
8. (US) Constitution
9. James Buchanan
10. executive
11. North Carolina
12. Massachusetts
13. *Lusitania*
14. James K. Polk
Bonus: Marbury v. Madison

PAGES 38-39:

1. b
2. United States
3. Abraham Lincoln
4. 3
5. (ancient) Egyptians (also accept: Egypt, Ancient Egypt)
6. Pacific
7. Thomas Jefferson
8. c
9. France
10. Sweden
11. Thomas Jefferson
12. Julius Caesar
13. South Carolina
14. Woodrow Wilson
Bonus: Francisco Pizarro

PAGES 40-41:

1. Tuesday
2. Iowa
3. false
4. Arctic Ocean
5. Gulf of Mexico (also accept: Atlantic Ocean)
6. Asia
7. false
8. Pandora

10. faun(s)
11. Korean War
12. Hillary Clinton
13. 1972
14. Shawnee
Bonus: Hannibal Hamlin

PAGES 42-43:

1. false
2. Vermont
3. false
4. Sahara
5. Alexander Graham Bell
6. c
7. March
8. Louisiana
9. William Howard Taft
10. Santa Fe (New Mexico)
11. Oregon
12. France
13. (income) tax evasion
14. Japan
Bonus: Colorado

PAGES 44-45:

1. true
2. 2
3. false
4. Greece
5. (ancient) Egyptians (also accept: Egypt, Ancient Egypt)
6. a
7. Library of Congress
8. a
9. c
10. Queen Elizabeth (also accept: Elizabeth I)
11. a

12. Rosa Parks (also accept: Rosa Louise McCauley)
13. Queen Elizabeth (also accept: Elizabeth I)
14. Wyoming
Bonus: January 3

PAGES 46-47:

1. Italy
2. November 25
3. b
4. b
5. (Dolley) Madison
6. Abraham Lincoln
7. Texas
8. Theodore Roosevelt
9. 8
10. Mongolia
11. Fort Knox
12. Warren Harding
13. France
14. England
Bonus: Pennsylvania

PAGES 48-49:

1. Yellowstone
2. Canada
3. true
4. Delaware
5. b
6. Chicago
7. b
8. coast guard (also accept: United States coast guard)
9. Eleanor Roosevelt
10. Air Force One
11. France
12. Grover Cleveland
13. Turkey
14. Russia
Bonus: Switzerland

PHOTO CREDITS

PENGUIN YOUNG READERS LICENSES

An Imprint of Penguin Random House LLC, New York

Penguin supports copyright. Copyright fuels creativity, encourages diverse voices, promotes free speech, and creates a vibrant culture. Thank you for buying an authorized edition of this book and for complying with copyright laws by not reproducing, scanning, or distributing any part of it in any form without permission. You are supporting writers and allowing Penguin to continue to publish books for every reader.

The publisher does not have any control over and does not assume any responsibility for author or third-party websites or their content.

MGM

ARE YOU SMARTER THAN A 5TH GRADER and all related logos and slogans TM & © 2007–2020 UAMG Content, LLC. ARE YOU SMARTER THAN A 5TH GRADER: History Class: A Companion Quiz Book © 2020 Metro-Goldwyn Mayer Studios Inc. All Rights Reserved.

METRO-GOLDWYN-MAYER is a trademark of Metro-Goldwyn-Mayer Lion Corp. © 2020 Metro-Goldwyn-Mayer Studios Inc. All Rights Reserved.

Nickelodeon is a trademark of Viacom International Inc.

Published in 2020 by Penguin Young Readers Licenses, an imprint of Penguin Random House LLC, New York. Manufactured in China.

Visit us online at www.penguinrandomhouse.com.

ISBN 9780593222393   10 9 8 7 6 5 4 3 2 1